FOOD BRANDS WE LOVE

KELLOGG'S

By Kaitlyn Duling

Kaleidoscope
Minneapolis, MN

The Quest for Discovery Never Ends

This edition is co-published by agreement between Kaleidoscope and World Book, Inc.

Kaleidoscope Publishing, Inc.
6012 Blue Circle Drive
Minnetonka, MN 55343 U.S.A.

World Book, Inc.
180 North LaSalle St., Suite 900
Chicago IL 60601 U.S.A.

Kaleidoscope ISBNs
978-1-64519-212-1 (library bound)
978-1-64519-280-0 (ebook)

World Book ISBN
978-0-7166-4190-2 (library bound)

Library of Congress Control Number
2020936211

Developed and produced by Focus Strategic Communications Inc.

Printed in the United States of America.

Bigfoot lurks within one of the images in this book. It's up to you to find him!

TABLE OF CONTENTS

Chapter 1
Breakfast Time

From deep within her sleep, Lin heard the buzz of her alarm. She rolled over in bed, fumbling for the phone. She had already hit the snooze icon a few times. If she did not want to be late for school, she had to get moving. Groggily, she threw on a pair of jeans and a t-shirt. She stuffed her feet into her favorite pair of sneakers. Her hair was still in yesterday's braid. It would have to do.

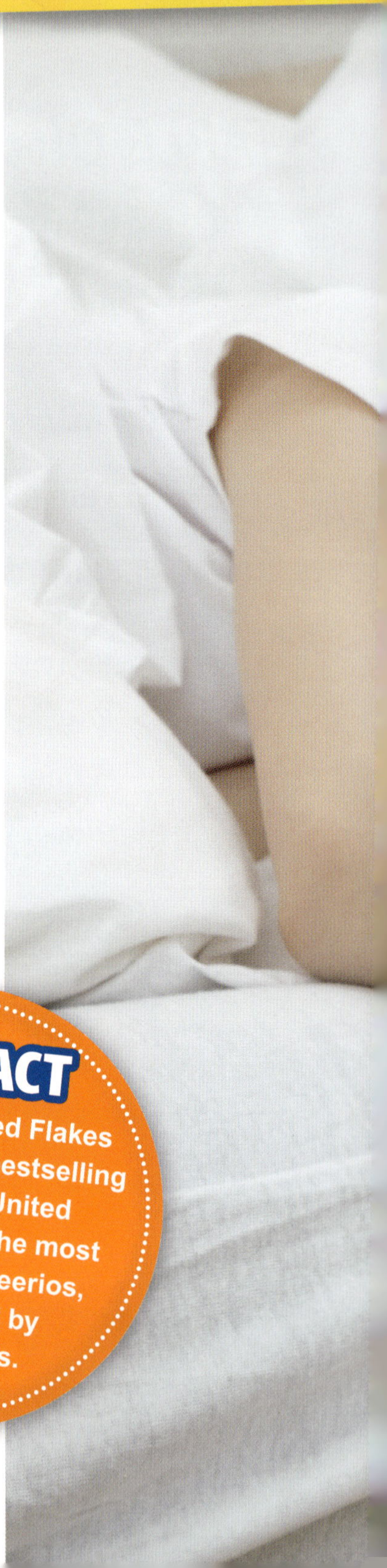

FUN FACT

Kellogg's Frosted Flakes was the second-bestselling cereal in the United States in 2019. The most popular was Cheerios, which is sold by General Mills.

Getting up in the morning is sometimes hard to do.

Pancakes are a favorite breakfast food for many people.

Downstairs, Lin's dad was making pancakes and bacon. He poured the batter onto the hot griddle. It crackled with heat. "Mmm, that smells great," Lin said. But she moved past her dad and looked through the cabinet. There it was—her favorite cereal bowl. It was round and blue. She fished her favorite spoon out of a drawer. She had just enough time for breakfast.

"You sure you don't want some?" Lin's dad asked. "You eat those Corn Flakes every single morning. How about changing it up?" Lin rolled her eyes. "They're my favorite." In the pantry, Lin pushed the Froot Loops, All-Bran, and Crispix aside. She barely glanced at the Pop-Tarts. Nutri-Grain bars were a no-go, too. Lin had her eyes on the prize: a big box of Corn Flakes.

FUN FACT

Kellogg's Corn Flakes have been around since 1906 when the company first opened. Twelve years earlier, the Kellogg brothers accidentally created Corn Flakes cereal.

Corn Flakes were created by J. H. Kellogg in 1894.

Corn Flakes and milk are a popular breakfast meal. Some people sprinkle sugar on top.

Pouring the cereal into her bowl, Lin looked at the clock. She would have to hurry to make it to school by 7:30 a.m. In the fridge, she found a carton of milk. She poured it over the flakes. Then, she added some dried banana chips. It was the perfect bowl of cereal. That is why Lin had eaten it every day since she was in third grade.

Over the years, Lin had tried plenty of other cereals. Most of them were the same **brand** as Corn Flakes. Kellogg's makes many types of breakfast foods and snacks. Lin's favorite was also the company's first **product**. She was not about to give up Corn Flakes, no matter how much her dad teased her. It was the very best way to start her day.

A bowl of Corn Flakes and milk is the start to many people's days.

Chapter 2

History of Kellogg's

The Kellogg Company was created by accident. Today, the brand is known around the world. People love to eat Kellogg's cereal. They eat it in just about every country on the planet. But it was not always a **global** company.

Kellogg's began in Battle Creek, Michigan. In the mid-1800s, a health spa was founded in Battle Creek. It was known as the Battle Creek Sanitarium. People came to the spa when they were sick. John Harvey, or J.H., Kellogg was a doctor there. His brother, Will Keith, or W.K., worked alongside him.

FUN FACT

Pop-Tarts were introduced in 1964. There were just four flavors: apple, strawberry, blueberry, and brown sugar cinnamon.

The Kellogg Sanitarium in Battle Creek, Michigan burned down in 1902.

For J. H. Kellogg, milk was an important part of a Corn Flake breakfast.

Kellogg's employed many women on their Corn Flakes assembly lines.

In 1894, the two brothers tried out some new recipes. They wanted to make a healthy granola. Some of the wheat was left out overnight. In the morning, they were surprised to find that the wheat was dry. They flattened it. They tasted it. It was good. They had invented the very first flaked cereal.

After that, there were more experiments. They tried other grains. The brothers finally landed on the recipe for the corn flake in 1898. A factory was built. Workers were hired. Finally, the two began to market the cereal in 1906. A brand was born. Corn Flakes quickly grew popular across the country.

Kellogg's **expanded** into Canada in 1914. In the years that followed, the brothers created many new products, such as Rice Krispies and Raisin Bran. W.K. Kellogg passed away in 1951 at the age of 91. The brand he built lives on. The Kellogg Company continues to experiment with new **ingredients** and products.

A 1948 magazine ad promoted Kellogg's cereals for breakfast.

KELLOGG'S BRAND TIMELINE

1906
W.K. Kellogg opens his first factory and creates Corn Flakes.

1914
Canada starts selling Corn Flakes for the first time.

1928
Kellogg's introduces Rice Krispies.

1930
W.K. Kellogg forms the W.K. Kellogg Foundation.

1933
The characters Snap, Crackle, and Pop appear in advertising.

1942
Raisin Bran comes to stores.

1963
Kellogg bring out Froot Loops.

1964
Pop-Tarts first come out.

1906 1914 1928 1930 1933 1942 1963 1964

1967
Frosted flavors hit shelves in 1967.

1995
Kellogg's begins to develop and sell packaged Rice Krispies Treats.

2001
Kellogg's buys the Keebler Foods Company. Keebler produces popular cookies and crackers.

2019
Kellogg's sells Keebler, along with Famous Amos, Murray's, and several other brands.

1967 1969 1995 1997 2001 2006 2012 2019

2006
The Kellogg Company celebrates its 100-year anniversary.

1997
The W.K. Kellogg Institute for Food and Nutrition Research opens.

2012
Kellogg's buys Pringles potato chips, making it the second-largest snack food company in the world.

1969
Kellogg's provides breakfast for the astronauts during the Apollo 11 trip to the moon.

Chapter 3

Cereal Box or Toy Box?

Jack's stomach rumbled. The smell was making his mouth water. Sticky marshmallow covered his hands. Tomorrow was Jack's birthday. He had promised his whole sixth grade class a treat. What could be better than Rice Krispies Treats? Jack's mom helped him heat the butter and melt the marshmallows. But Jack did most of the steps. It was fun to cook with cereal.

Rice Krispies Treats were invented in 1927. The original recipe included cereal, butter, molasses, and vinegar. The treats became popular after a Campfire Girls troop sold them as a fundraiser. The recipe was added to the back of the Rice Krispies box in 1941.

Making Rice Krispies Treats starts with melting the butter.

Rice Krispies, butter, and marshmallows are used to make Rice Krispie Treats.

Snap, Crackle, and Pop first appeared on Kellogg's packages in 1933.

Rice Krispies were Jack's favorite cereal. He remembered looking at the box when he was younger. The characters—Snap, Crackle, and Pop—were cute and fun. If he thought about it, Jack could name tons of Kellogg's cereal **mascots**.

Dig'em Frog was the mascot for Honey Smacks beginning in 1972.

There was Sunny the Sun from Raisin Bran. Toucan Sam sold Froot Loops. Dig 'Em Frog had been the mascot of Honey Smacks for decades. And who could forget Tony the Tiger? Jack always saw Tony on commercials for Frosted Flakes.

THEY'RE GRRREAT!

The Frosted Flake's mascot is Tony the Tiger. He first appeared on cereal boxes in 1952. To become the mascot, Tony had to win a popularity contest. Kellogg's printed boxes with four different characters. There was Katy the Kangaroo, Elmo the Elephant, and Newt the Gnu. Cereal fans voted. They chose Tony! Since then, he has become a beloved part of the brand. In Mexico, he is known as Tigre Tono. In France, his name is Tony Le Tigre.

The mascots were just one part of the fun. Jack's mom motioned to the box of cereal. "When I was young, Kellogg's cereal always had the coolest prizes," she said. From the 1960s to the early 2000s, cereal boxes often had plastic toys inside.

Light-up spoons, plastic whistles, and tiny boats were just a few of the options. Cereal box prizes are rare today. But kids still love cereal. Jack loved the colorful mascots, the bright boxes, and the crunchy, sweet cereals.

Kellogg's makes a wide variety of breakfast cereals.

FUN FACT

Corn Flakes was the very first cereal to come with a prize. Customers were handed the *Funny Jungleland Moving Pictures Booklet* when they purchased a box of cereal. Later, the booklet became a mail-in offer. The prize offer ran all the way from 1909 to 1937. Over the years, millions of books were given away.

Chapter 4
Bowl of Dreams

Mona was not a fan of cereal, but she loved to eat Pop-Tarts. She could eat them for breakfast. She could eat them as a snack. Sometimes, she ate them for dessert.

Looking around the kitchen, Mona could see plenty of Kellogg's products. Some were cereals. But many were not. Kellogg's sells waffles and protein bars. It sells shakes and crackers. The company is famous for breakfast. But it has worked hard to expand.

CEREAL TOWN

Battle Creek, Michigan has long been known as cereal central. For several years, there were more than 100 different cereal companies located in Battle Creek. Today, Post, Kellogg's, and Ralston Foods call Battle Creek home.

Frozen Eggo Waffles first appeared on grocery shelves in the 1950s.

Kellogg's has manufacturing plants in 18 countries around the world.

If she traveled the world, Mona could find her favorite foods in other countries, too. Kellogg's products are available in more than 180 countries. To keep up with **demand**, Kellogg's built more factories. There are now Kellogg's factories around the world.

Some cereals are not made in the United States. You can only find them in their home countries or on the internet. Mona would have to go to South Africa to

Rose Badam Corn Flakes are produced in India with real roses and almonds.

try Strawberry Pops. She could try Vector in Canada. India is home to Corn Flakes cereals flavored with rose, saffron, and mango. That is some serious world traveling.

FUN FACT

Kellogg's sales were about $13 billion in 2018.

KELLOGG'S

BRANDS

CEREALS

Corn Flakes
Froot Loops
Frosted Flakes
Frosted Mini Wheats
Happy Inside
Krave
Raisin Bran
Rice Krispies
Special K

PASTRIES/ BARS

Pop-Tarts
Eggo Frozen Breakfast
Special K Bars
Special K Beverages
Special K Crackers
Nutri-Grain Bars

Kellogg's products are popular at food banks around the world.

Kellogg's makes more than tasty cereal and snacks. The company tries to make a difference, too. They partner with **food banks** around the world. Since 2013, Kellogg's has provided more than 3 billion servings of food to people in need. Kellogg's also supports school breakfast programs and donates money to charities. Between 2014 and 2018, Kellogg's donated more than $270 million in money and products.

For more than 100 years, Kellogg's has grown and changed. Corn Flakes were first, and the company still sells plenty of them. But Kellogg's now offers more options and flavors than ever before. What will they think of next? Only time will tell.

BEYOND

THE BOOK

After reading the book, it's time to think about what you learned. Try the following exercises to jumpstart your ideas.

THINK

THAT'S NEWS TO ME. Kellogg's is always introducing new products, flavors, and ideas. Consider how you learn about new foods and brands. What information can be found in news articles? What about news programs on TV? Where can you go to find news you can trust?

CREATE

PRIMARY SOURCES. Primary sources provide firsthand accounts of an event. Interviews, videos, and photographs are all examples of primary sources. Create a list of the kinds of primary sources you might be able to find about Kellogg's.

SHARE

WHAT'S YOUR OPINION? The text states that the Kellogg Company makes a difference. Do you agree with that statement? Provide evidence from the text to support your opinion. Share your position and evidence with a friend. Does your friend find the argument convincing?

GROW

DRAWING CONNECTIONS. Create a diagram that shows and explains connections between the different products Kellogg's makes. How does learning about the products help you better understand Kellogg's?

RESEARCH NINJA

Visit www.ninjaresearcher.com/2121 to learn how to take your research skills and book report writing to the next level!

RESEARCH

DIGITAL LITERACY TOOLS

SEARCH LIKE A PRO

Learn how to use search engines to find useful websites.

FACT OR FAKE?

Discover how you can tell a trusted website from an untrustworthy resource.

TEXT DETECTIVE

Explore how to zero in on the information you need most.

SHOW YOUR WORK

Research responsibly—learn how to cite sources.

WRITE

GET TO THE POINT

Learn how to express your main ideas.

PLAN OF ATTACK

Learn prewriting exercises and create an outline.

DOWNLOADABLE REPORT FORMS

Further Resources

BOOKS

Green, Sara. *General Mills*. Hopkins, MN: Bellwether Media, 2018.

Green, Sara. *Kellogg's*. Hopkins, MN: Bellwether Media, 2015.

McGinty, Alice B. *Pancakes to Parathas: Breakfast Around the World*. New York, NY: Little Bee Books, 2019.

Parker, Vic. *Grains*. New York, NY: Quarto Publishing Group USA, 2016.

WEBSITES

FACTSURFER

Factsurfer.com gives you a safe, fun way to find more information.

1. Go to www.factsurfer.com.
2. Enter "Kellogg's" into the search box and click
3. Select your book cover to see a list of related websites.

Glossary

brand: The name of a product made by a company.

demand: The amount of something that customers buy and eat.

expanded: Made something grow, widen, or increase, such as a company's share of a market.

food banks: Places where food is supplied for free to people in need.

global: Relating to the entire world, as in a worldwide company.

ingredients: The individual parts of something, such as the foods or spices in a recipe or dish.

mascots: Characters or symbols that represent a brand or organization.

product: Something that is made to be sold, such as processed foods.

Index

PHOTO CREDITS

The images in this book are reproduced through the courtesy of: Tiger Images/Shutterstock Images, front cover (waffles); Sheila Fitzgerald/Shutterstock Images, front cover (Eggo waffles), pp. 4, 19, 26 (Special K snack bar); DenisMArt/Shutterstock Images, front cover (Rice Krispies), pp. 3, 20 (bottom), 26 (Nutri Grain bar); PHIL LENOIR/Shutterstock Images, front cover (cereal bowl), p. 31; calimedia/Shutterstock Images, front cover (Kellogg's Fun Pak), p. 26 (Mini Wheats); Hong Vo/Shutterstock Images, pp. 1, 14 (top right); foxaon1987/ Shutterstock Images, p. 1 (background); Andrey_Popov/Shutterstock Images, pp. 4-5; CKP1001/Shutterstock Images, p. 6; Lunasee Studios/Shutterstock Images, pp. 7, 15 (top right); Nitr/Shutterstock Images, p. 8; MAHATHIR MOHD YASIN/Shutterstock Images, p. 9; Evan-Amos/CC BY-SA 3.0, pp. 10, 26 (Pop Tarts); Gage Printing Co., printer/Public Domain, p. 11 (top); Bettmann/Getty Images, p. 11 (bottom); National Archives and Records Administration, p. 12; Internet Archive Book Images, p. 13; urbanbuzz/Shutterstock Images, pp. 14 (top left), 26 (Rice Krispies); Sara Stathas/Alamy Stock Photo, p. 14 (bottom); Keith Homan/Shutterstock Images, p. 15 (top left); MAHATHIR MOHD YASIN/Shutterstock Images, p. 15 (bottom); knelson20/Shutterstock Images, pp. 16-17 (top); Marcie Fowler – Shining Hope Images/Shutterstock Images, pp. 16 -17 (bottom); Tim Boyle/Hulton Archive/Getty Images, p. 18 (top); Kristoffer Tripplaar/Alamy Stock Photo, p. 18 (bottom); Roland Magnusson/Shutterstock Images, p. 20 (top); Amoret Tanner/Alamy Stock Photo, p. 21; KK Stock/Shutterstock Images, p. 23 (top); JJava Designs/Shutterstock Images, p. 23 (Eggo waffles); trabantos/Shutterstock Images, p. 24; bhavit chawla/Shutterstock Images, p. 25 (top); ElenaR/Shutterstock Images, p. 25 (bottom); George W. Bailey/Shutterstock Images, p. 26 (Corn Flakes); HASPhotos/Shutterstock Images, p. 27.

About the Author

Kaitlyn Duling loves to eat cereal for breakfast. She has written more than 100 books for children. She lives in Washington, D.C.